foreword

Whether you love the crunch of tender-crisp bell peppers or the fresh bursts of colour they offer, this collection of favourite pepper recipes from Company's Coming is sure to appeal.

Judging by their naturally vibrant colours, you'd think bell peppers have the power to stop traffic with their green, yellow and red hues—and don't forget gorgeous orange peppers, and the more unusual heirloom varieties that can be purple or even chocolate brown!

Bell peppers are beloved for adding not only pops of colour but also nutrition, as they're one of the best sources of vitamin C. No matter how you stuff, slice or dice them, peppers add a punch to many meals, including stir-fries, soups and both meat and vegetarian dishes. It's time to rediscover the power of peppers!

Jean Paré

onion pepper pizzettes

Peppers and caramelized onions come together to create mini-pizza appetizers that manage to be both cute and sophisticated.

Olive (or cooking) oil	1 1/2 tsp.	7 mL
Diced onion	1 cup	250 mL
Roasted red peppers, drained, blotted dry and chopped	3/4 cup	175 mL
Red wine vinegar	1 tsp.	5 mL
Salt	1/8 tsp.	0.5 mL
Pepper	1/8 tsp.	0.5 mL
Basil pesto	1/4 cup	60 mL
Unbaked pizza crust (12 inch, 30 cm, diameter)	1	1
Goat (chèvre) cheese, cut up	2 1/2 oz.	70 g

Heat olive oil in large frying pan on medium. Add onion. Cook for about 15 minutes, stirring often, until caramelized.

Add next 4 ingredients. Stir. Remove from heat.

Spread pesto on pizza crust. Cut out circles with 2 inch (5 cm) round cookie cutter. Arrange on greased baking sheet with sides. Spoon onion mixture onto rounds.

Sprinkle with cheese. Bake in 400°F (205°C) oven for about 12 minutes until cheese is melted and just golden. Makes about 30 pizzettes.

1 pizzette: 43 Calories; 1.9 g Total Fat (0.7 g Mono, 0.2 g Poly, 0.6 g Sat); 2 mg Cholesterol; 5 g Carbohydrate; trace Fibre; 1 g Protein; 68 mg Sodium

red peppered chorizo

You're only five ingredients away from making this delicious spread!
Conveniently made in the slow cooker, it has fantastic flavour that
goes great on baguette, crackers or crostini.

Uncooked Chorizo (or hot Italian) sausage, casing removed	1 1/2 lbs.	680 g
Jar of roasted red peppers, drained and chopped	12 oz.	340 mL
Balsamic vinaigrette dressing	2 tbsp.	30 mL
Frozen concentrated orange juice, thawed	2 tbsp.	30 mL
Goat (chèvre) cheese	1/3 cup	75 mL

Scramble-fry sausage in large frying pan on medium-high for about
12 minutes until no longer pink. Drain. Transfer to 3 1/2 to 4 quart (3.5 to
4 L) slow cooker.

Add next 3 ingredients. Stir. Cook, covered, on Low for 3 to 4 hours or on
High for 1 1/2 to 2 hours.

Add cheese. Stir until melted. Makes about 2 1/2 cups (625 mL).

1/4 cup (60 mL): 304 Calories; 20.2 g Total Fat (8.5 g Mono, 2.3 g Poly, 7.6 g Sat);
42 mg Cholesterol; 11 g Carbohydrate; trace Fibre; 16 g Protein; 1191 mg Sodium

shrimp-stuffed peppers

Appetizing shrimp served in green pepper boats. These convenient appetizers can be made ahead and reheated in the microwave when you're ready for them.

Uncooked shrimp (peeled and deveined), blotted dry and finely chopped	6 oz.	170 g
Cornstarch	1 tbsp.	15 mL
Dry sherry	2 tsp.	10 mL
Green onion, finely sliced	1	1
Garlic powder, sprinkle		
Ground ginger, sprinkle		
Medium green peppers, cut lengthwise into 6 pieces each	2	2
Black bean sauce (pourable)	1/2 cup	125 mL

Combine first 6 ingredients in small bowl.

Spoon about 2 tsp. (10 mL) shrimp mixture onto each green pepper piece, packing down slightly. Set in large bamboo steamer or on rack over rapidly boiling water in wok or Dutch oven. Cover. Steam for 6 to 7 minutes until peppers are tender-crisp and shrimp mixture turns pink. Add more boiling water to wok or pot as required to keep water boiling rapidly.

Drizzle with black bean sauce. Makes 12 pieces.

2 pieces: 73 Calories; 2.1 g Total Fat (1 g Mono, 0.7 g Poly, 0.2 g Sat); 32 mg Cholesterol; 8 g Carbohydrate; 1 g Fibre; 6 g Protein; 851 mg Sodium

roasted red pepper dip

This versatile dip can be paired with cocktail meatballs, a cheese platter, or even spread on slices of toasted baguette. Sherry vinegar adds an authentic Spanish flavour, but white wine vinegar could be substituted.

Olive oil	2 tbsp.	30 mL
Finely chopped onion	1/3 cup	75 mL
Garlic cloves, minced (or 3/4 tsp., 4 mL, powder)	3	3
Dried crushed chilies	1/2 tsp.	2 mL
Can of navy beans, rinsed and drained	14 oz.	398 mL
Roasted red peppers	1 1/2 cups	375 mL
Tomato paste (see Tip, page 64)	2 tbsp.	30 mL
Sherry vinegar	1 tbsp.	15 mL
Chopped fresh rosemary (or 1/4 tsp., 1 mL, dried, crushed), optional	1 tsp.	5 mL
Salt	1/4 tsp.	1 mL
Chopped fresh parsley (or 3/4 tsp., 4 mL, flakes)	1 tbsp.	15 mL

Heat olive oil in small frying pan on medium. Add next 3 ingredients. Cook for about 5 minutes, stirring often, until onion is softened.

Put next 6 ingredients into food processor. Add onion mixture. Process with on/off motion until almost smooth. Transfer to shallow medium bowl.

Sprinkle with parsley. Cool to room temperature. Makes about 3 cups (750 mL).

1/2 cup (125 mL): 160 Calories; 5.6 g Total Fat (3.4 g Mono, 0.5 g Poly, 0.7 g Sat); 0 mg Cholesterol; 22 g Carbohydrate; 6 g Fibre; 6 g Protein; 633 mg Sodium

grilled peperonata

Peperonata (pronounced pehp-uh-roh-NAH-tah) is an Italian mixture of peppers and onions. This version can be enjoyed with grilled meats or even tossed with pasta.

Olive oil	3 tbsp.	50 mL
Chopped fresh rosemary	2 tsp.	10 mL
Garlic cloves, minced	2	2
Large red onion, thickly sliced	1	1
Medium green pepper, halved	1	1
Medium red pepper, halved	1	1
Medium orange pepper, halved	1	1
Medium yellow pepper, halved	1	1
Balsamic vinegar	2 tbsp.	30 mL
Chopped fresh parsley	1 tbsp.	15 mL

Combine first 3 ingredients in small bowl. Let stand at room temperature for 30 minutes to blend flavours.

Preheat electric grill to high. Brush onion and peppers with olive oil mixture. Cook on lightly greased grill for 6 to 8 minutes, turning occasionally and brushing with olive oil mixture, until vegetables are tender-crisp. Transfer vegetables to cutting board. Cut into 3/4 inch (2 cm) pieces. Transfer to large bowl.

Add vinegar. Toss. Add parsley. Toss. Makes about 6 cups (1.5 L).

1/2 cup (125 mL): 53 Calories; 3.5 g Total Fat (2.5 g Mono, 0 g Poly, 0 g Sat); 0 mg Cholesterol; 5 g Carbohydrate; 1 g Fibre; trace Protein; 2 mg Sodium

roasted pepper ring

Bread rings are both impressive and delicious. This biscuit version has tangy roasted red pepper flavour baked right in.

All-purpose flour	3 cups	750 mL
Baking powder	2 tbsp.	30 mL
Dried oregano	1/2 tsp.	2 mL
Paprika	1/2 tsp.	2 mL
Salt	1/2 tsp.	2 mL
Pepper	1/4 tsp.	1 mL
Garlic powder	1/4 tsp.	1 mL
Cold butter (or hard margarine)	1/2 cup	125 mL
Buttermilk (or soured milk, see Tip, page 64)	1 cup	250 mL
Roasted red peppers, drained and blotted dry, finely chopped	1/2 cup	125 mL
Butter (or hard margarine), melted	2 tbsp.	30 mL
Garlic powder	1/2 tsp.	2 mL
Paprika	1/4 tsp.	1 mL
Grated sharp Cheddar cheese	1/4 cup	60 mL

Measure first 7 ingredients into large bowl. Stir. Cut in first amount of butter until mixture resembles coarse crumbs. Make a well in centre.

Add buttermilk and red pepper to well. Stir until soft dough forms. Turn out onto lightly floured surface. Knead 8 times. Roll or pat out to 3/4 inch (2 cm) thickness. Cut out circles with lightly floured 2 1/2 inch (6.4 cm) biscuit cutter.

Combine next 3 ingredients in small bowl. Brush tops with half of butter mixture. Arrange circles, standing on sides with inner edges touching to keep upright, in circular pattern in greased 9 inch (23 cm) pie plate. Bake in 375°F (190°C) oven for 20 minutes.

Sprinkle with cheese. Bake for another 20 minutes until cheese is golden and wooden pick inserted in ring comes out clean. Brush with remaining butter mixture. Let stand for 5 minutes. Cuts into 12 pieces.

1 piece: 232 Calories; 11.4 g Total Fat (3.2 g Mono, 0.6 g Poly, 6.7 g Sat); 31 mg Cholesterol; 28 g Carbohydrate; 1 g Fibre; 5 g Protein; 426 mg Sodium

hot pepper jelly

Spicy pepper jelly served with any type of cheese makes a fabulous appetizer. Don't be shy to experiment! Try spooning it over cream cheese and pairing with crackers. Use green peppers for a green tint and red peppers for an orange-red colour.

Chopped green (or red) pepper	1 1/2 cups	375 mL
Chopped canned jalapeño pepper	1/4 cup	60 mL
White vinegar	1 1/2 cups	375 mL
Granulated sugar	6 1/2 cups	1.6 L
Liquid pectin (see Note 1)	6 oz.	170 mL
Green liquid food colouring (optional)		

Measure first 3 ingredients into blender. Process until smooth. Transfer to large pot.

Add sugar. Heat and stir on medium-high until sugar is dissolved. Bring to a boil. Boil for 3 minutes.

Stir in pectin. Bring to a hard boil. Boil hard for 1 minute. Remove from heat. Skim and discard foam.

Add food colouring to make a darker green. Stir. Fill 6 hot sterile 1 cup (250 mL) jars to within 1/4 inch (6 mm) of top. Remove air bubbles and adjust headspace if necessary. Wipe rims. Place hot metal lids on jars and screw on metal bands fingertip tight. Do not over-tighten. Process in boiling water bath for 10 minutes (see Note 2). Remove jars. Let stand at room temperature until cool. Refrigerate after opening. Makes about 6 cups (1.5 L).

1 tbsp. (15 mL): 51 Calories; 0 g Total Fat (0 g Mono, 0 g Poly, 0 g Sat); 0 mg Cholesterol; 13 g Carbohydrate; 0 g Fibre; 0 g Protein; 6 mg Sodium

Note 1: Instructions for using liquid pectin vary by brand. Please follow the manufacturer's instructions on the package you are using.

Note 2: Processing time is for elevations 1001 to 3000 feet (306 to 915 m) above sea level. Make adjustment for elevation in your area if necessary.

pepper and onion refrigerator pickles

These colourful and versatile pickled onions and peppers are perfect for serving as a condiment with barbecued burgers.

Large onion, cut into very thin slices	1	1
Cold water, to cover		
Large green pepper, sliced into rings	1	1
Large red pepper, sliced into rings	1	1
Large yellow pepper, sliced into rings	1	1
Granulated sugar	1 1/3 cups	325 mL
Water	1 1/3 cups	325 mL
White vinegar	1 1/3 cups	325 mL
Cooking oil	2 tbsp.	30 mL

Separate onion slices into rings. Place in large bowl. Cover with cold water. Let stand for 1 hour. Drain.

Add next 3 ingredients.

Combine remaining 4 ingredients in medium saucepan. Bring to a boil on medium. Stir until sugar dissolves. Remove from heat. Pour over onion mixture. Chill, covered, for at least 24 hours before serving. Serves 10.

1 serving: 150 Calories; 3.0 g Total Fat (1.5 g Mono, 1.0 g Poly, 0 g Sat); 0 mg Cholesterol; 33 g Carbohydrate; 1 g Fibre; trace Protein; 2 mg Sodium

green pepper steak

Let the oven do most of the work! This light dish is very simple to put together, and then all it needs is time to bake.

Boneless beef round steak, trimmed of fat and cut into thin strips	1 1/2 lbs.	680 g
Sliced fresh white mushrooms	2 cups	500 mL
Can of diced tomatoes (with juice)	14 oz.	398 mL
Can of condensed onion soup	10 oz.	284 mL
Large green pepper, cut into thin strips	1	1
Thinly sliced onion	1/2 cup	125 mL
Low-sodium soy sauce	1 tbsp.	15 mL
Pepper	1/8 tsp.	0.5 mL

Spray medium frying pan with cooking spray. Add steak. Cook on medium-high for about 2 minutes, stirring often, until browned. Transfer to 2 quart (2 L) casserole.

Combine remaining 7 ingredients in large bowl. Add to steak. Stir. Cook, covered, in 350°F (175°C) oven for 1 1/2 to 2 hours until steak is very tender. Makes about 5 cups (1.25 L).

1 cup (250 mL): 253 Calories; 9.0 g Total Fat (3.5 g Mono, 1.0 g Poly, 3.0 g Sat); 80 mg Cholesterol; 11 g Carbohydrate; 2 g Fibre; 32 g Protein; 933 mg Sodium

mango pepper patties

Bright red peppers and a tasty mango salsa add a touch of class to ordinary beef patties for a fabulous weeknight dinner.

Large red peppers, halved crosswise	2	2
Diced ripe mango	1 cup	250 mL
Thinly sliced green onion	1/4 cup	60 mL
Apple cider vinegar	1 tbsp.	15 mL
Granulated sugar	1 tbsp.	15 mL
Cooking oil	2 tsp.	10 mL
Salt	1/8 tsp.	0.5 mL
Pepper, just a pinch		
Large egg, fork-beaten	1	1
Finely chopped onion	1/2 cup	125 mL
Graham cracker crumbs	1/2 cup	125 mL
Chili paste (sambal oelek)	1 tbsp.	15 mL
Salt	1/4 tsp.	1 mL
Lean ground beef	1 lb.	454 g

Cut one 1 1/2 inch (3.8 cm) ring from each red pepper half, for a total of 4 rings. Set aside. Finely chop remaining red pepper. Put into medium bowl.

Add next 7 ingredients. Stir.

Combine next 5 ingredients in large bowl. Add ground beef. Mix well. Divide into 4 equal portions. Place 1 portion inside each red pepper ring. Flatten into patties to fill rings. Preheat gas barbecue to medium. Cook patties on greased grill for about 10 minutes per side until internal temperature reaches 160°F (71°C). Serve with mango mixture. Serves 4.

1 serving: 338 Calories; 14.8 g Total Fat (6.7 g Mono, 1.5 g Poly, 4.7 g Sat); 111 mg Cholesterol; 28 g Carbohydrate; 3 g Fibre; 24 g Protein; 372 mg Sodium

saucy short ribs

Make it a rib night! Tender ribs and tasty sauce are baked with plenty of peppers and onions.

Beef short ribs, bone-in, cut into 1-bone portions	3 lbs.	1.4 kg
Water	1/2 cup	125 mL
Large green peppers, sliced	2	2
Large Spanish onion, sliced	1	1
Sliced fresh white mushrooms	1 lb.	454 g
Jar of sliced pimiento	2 oz.	57 mL
Cans of condensed beef broth (10 oz., 284 mL, each)	2	2
Can of tomato paste	5 1/2 oz.	156 mL
All-purpose flour	2 tbsp.	30 mL
Worcestershire sauce	2 tbsp.	30 mL
Dried oregano	1/2 tsp.	2 mL
Salt	1/4 tsp.	1 mL
Pepper	1/8 tsp.	0.5 mL
Cayenne pepper	1/4 tsp.	1 mL

Place ribs in large roasting pan. Add water. Cook, covered, in 350°F (175°C) oven for 2 hours. Drain.

Cover ribs with next 4 ingredients.

Combine remaining 8 ingredients in medium bowl. Mix well. Pour over ribs. Cook, covered, for 1 hour, stirring occasionally. Serves 6.

1 serving: 480 Calories; 25.0 g Total Fat (10.0 g Mono, 1.0 g Poly, 10.0 g Sat); 110 mg Cholesterol; 13 g Carbohydrate; 3 g Fibre; 51 g Protein; 1150 mg Sodium

stuffed peppers

These classic stuffed peppers are prepared in the slow cooker for maximum flavour with minimal effort.

Boiling water	1/4 cup	60 mL
Instant white rice	1/4 cup	60 mL
Lean ground beef	1/2 lb.	225 g
Finely chopped onion	1/4 cup	60 mL
Frozen kernel corn	1/4 cup	60 mL
Grated carrot	1/4 cup	60 mL
Prepared horseradish	1/2 tsp.	2 mL
Worcestershire sauce	1/2 tsp.	2 mL
Salt	1/2 tsp.	2 mL
Pepper	1/8 tsp.	0.5 mL
Medium green peppers	4	4
Can of condensed tomato soup	10 oz.	284 mL

Pour boiling water over rice in medium heatproof bowl. Let stand, covered, for 5 minutes.

Add next 8 ingredients. Mix well.

Cut 1/2 inch (12 mm) from top of each green pepper. Remove seeds and ribs. Stuff with rice mixture. Place in 5 quart (5 L) slow cooker.

Spoon soup over top and around peppers. Cook, covered, on Low for 7 to 9 hours or on High for 3 1/2 to 4 1/2 hours. Serves 4.

1 serving: 192 Calories; 4.0 g Total Fat (1.5 g Mono, 0.5 g Poly, 2.0 g Sat); 35 mg Cholesterol; 26 g Carbohydrate; 4 g Fibre; 16 g Protein; 687 mg Sodium

easy teriyaki chicken pasta

Flavourful and simple to put together, with from-scratch teriyaki sauce.

Low-sodium soy sauce	1/3 cup	75 mL
Brown sugar, packed	3 tbsp.	50 mL
Garlic cloves, minced	2	2
Grated ginger root	1/2 tsp.	2 mL
Boneless, skinless chicken breast halves (about 3), thinly sliced	3/4 lb.	340 g
Cooking oil	1 tsp.	5 mL
Can of pineapple tidbits, drained and juice reserved	14 oz.	398 mL
Can of sliced water chestnuts, drained	8 oz.	227 mL
Medium red pepper, diced	1	1
Medium yellow pepper, diced	1	1
Cornstarch	2 tbsp.	30 mL
Reserved juice from pineapple		
Fresh bean sprouts (about 6 oz., 170 g)	2 1/2 cups	625 mL
Green onions, thinly sliced	3	3
Water	12 cups	3 L
Salt	1 1/2 tsp.	7 mL
Angel hair pasta	10 oz.	285 g

Combine first 4 ingredients in small cup. Stir until sugar is dissolved. Put chicken into medium bowl. Pour 3 tbsp. (50 mL) soy sauce mixture over chicken. Stir until coated. Let stand for 10 minutes.

Heat cooking oil in large frying pan on medium-high. Add chicken. Cook for 2 minutes. Add next 4 ingredients. Stir. Cook, covered, for about 3 minutes until peppers are tender-crisp. Make a well in centre.

Combine cornstarch, pineapple juice and remaining soy sauce mixture in small bowl. Pour into centre of chicken mixture. Sprinkle bean sprouts and green onion over top. Do not stir. Cook, covered, for about 2 minutes until boiling and thickened. Mix well.

Combine water and salt in Dutch oven. Bring to a boil. Add pasta. Boil, uncovered, for 5 to 6 minutes, stirring occasionally, until tender but firm. Drain. Transfer pasta to serving platter. Serve chicken mixture over top. Serves 6.

1 serving: 383 Calories; 3.0 g Total Fat (0.5 g Mono, 0.5 g Poly, 0 g Sat); 33 mg Cholesterol; 66 g Carbohydrate; 4 g Fibre; 24 g Protein; 582 mg Sodium

grilled pepper chicken

If it's too cold to barbecue, the chicken and peppers can be placed on a greased broiling pan and broiled on the top rack in the oven for about five minutes per side until the chicken is no longer pink inside.

Boneless, skinless chicken breast halves (4 – 6 oz., 113 g – 170 g, each)	4	4
Salt, sprinkle		
Pepper, sprinkle		
Small red pepper, quartered lengthwise	1	1
Small orange pepper, quartered lengthwise	1	1
Small yellow pepper, quartered lengthwise	1	1
Olive oil	1 tbsp.	15 mL
Dried oregano	1/2 tsp.	2 mL
Pepper, sprinkle		
Balsamic vinegar	2 tbsp.	30 mL
Crumbled light feta cheese	1/4 cup	60 mL
Finely chopped fresh parsley	2 tsp.	10 mL

Sprinkle chicken with salt and pepper. Preheat gas barbecue to medium-high. Cook chicken on greased grill for about 3 minutes per side until no longer pink inside.

Put next 3 ingredients into large bowl. Drizzle with olive oil. Sprinkle with oregano and pepper. Toss well. Cook peppers on grill for about 3 minutes per side until tender-crisp.

Transfer chicken and peppers to large bowl. Drizzle with balsamic vinegar. Toss. Transfer to large plate. Sprinkle with cheese and parsley. Serves 4.

1 serving: 196 Calories; 6.5 g Total Fat (3.0 g Mono, 0.8 g Poly, 1.7 g Sat); 68 mg Cholesterol; 6 g Carbohydrate; 1 g Fibre; 28 g Protein; 201 mg Sodium

the best chicken dish

An outstanding slow cooker meal that's perfect served with rice or pasta. It can be prepared the night before by browning the ground chicken, chopping the veggies and refrigerating everything in separate containers for easy assembly in the morning.

Cooking oil	1 tbsp.	15 mL
Lean ground chicken	1 lb.	454 g
Can of chickpeas (garbanzo beans), rinsed and drained	19 oz.	540 mL
Finely chopped onion	1 cup	250 mL
Salt	1/4 tsp.	1 mL
Sun-dried tomato pesto	1/3 cup	75 mL
All-purpose flour	1 tbsp.	15 mL
Can of diced tomatoes (with juice)	14 oz.	398 mL
Balsamic vinegar	1 tbsp.	15 mL
Granulated sugar	1/2 tsp.	2 mL
Salt	1/4 tsp.	1 mL
Chopped red pepper	4 cups	1 L
Finely chopped zucchini (with peel)	1 cup	250 mL

Heat cooking oil in large frying pan on medium. Add ground chicken. Scramble-fry for 5 to 10 minutes until no longer pink. Drain. Transfer to 3 1/2 to 4 quart (3.5 to 4 L) slow cooker.

Add next 3 ingredients. Stir.

Stir pesto into flour in medium bowl until smooth. Add next 4 ingredients. Stir well. Pour over chicken mixture. Stir well. Cook, covered, on Low for 8 to 10 hours or on High for 4 to 5 hours.

Add red pepper and zucchini. Stir. Cook, covered, on High for 30 to 45 minutes until red pepper is tender-crisp. Serves 8.

1 serving: 232 Calories; 11.2 g Total Fat (1.6 g Mono, 1.1 g Poly, 0.4 g Sat); 0 mg Cholesterol; 20 g Carbohydrate; 4 g Fibre; 14 g Protein; 353 mg Sodium

pepper chicken kabobs

No one would turn down sizzling kabobs hot off the grill—especially these tender pepper and chicken morsels marinated in a delicious citrus blend.

Boneless, skinless chicken breast halves, cut into 24 equal pieces	1 lb.	454 g
Medium onion, cut into 24 equal pieces	1	1
Large yellow pepper, cut into 24 equal pieces	1	1
Large red pepper, cut into 24 equal pieces	1	1
Bamboo skewers (8 inches, 20 cm, each), soaked in water for 10 minutes	8	8
Orange juice	1/2 cup	125 mL
Ranch dressing	1/4 cup	60 mL
Garlic cloves, minced (or 1/2 tsp., 2 mL, powder)	2	2
Grated lime zest	2 tsp.	10 mL
Ground cumin	1 tsp.	5 mL
Pepper	1 tsp.	5 mL

Thread first 4 ingredients alternately onto skewers. Place in large shallow dish.

Combine remaining 6 ingredients in small bowl. Pour about 2/3 cup (150 mL) over chicken skewers. Chill remaining orange juice mixture. Turn skewers to coat. Let stand, covered, in refrigerator for 2 hours, turning occasionally. Preheat gas barbecue to medium-high. Remove skewers from orange juice mixture. Discard any orange juice mixture remaining in dish. Cook skewers on greased grill for about 6 minutes per side, brushing with reserved orange juice mixture, until chicken is no longer pink inside and vegetables are tender. Serves 4.

1 serving: 225 Calories; 7.5 g Total Fat (0.5 g Mono, 0.5 g Poly, 1.4 g Sat); 69 mg Cholesterol; 12 g Carbohydrate; 2 g Fibre; 27 g Protein; 164 mg Sodium

rosemary turkey scaloppine

This is a recipe for those occasions when you really want to impress. Appetizing turkey scaloppine is presented atop colourful peppers and zucchini.

Finely chopped fresh rosemary (or 1/2 tsp., 2 mL, dried, crushed)	2 tsp.	10 mL
Salt	1/4 tsp.	1 mL
Pepper	1/4 tsp.	1 mL
Turkey scaloppine, halved crosswise	1 lb.	454 g
Cooking (or olive) oil	1 tbsp.	15 mL
Cooking (or olive) oil	1 tbsp.	15 mL
Chopped Asian eggplant (with peel)	1 cup	250 mL
Chopped zucchini (with peel)	1 cup	250 mL
Sliced green pepper	1 cup	250 mL
Sliced onion	1 cup	250 mL
Sliced red pepper	1 cup	250 mL
Sliced yellow pepper	1 cup	250 mL
Balsamic vinegar	1 tbsp.	15 mL
Chopped fresh rosemary (or 1/2 tsp., 2 mL, dried, crushed)	2 tsp.	10 mL
Salt	1/2 tsp.	2 mL
Pepper	1/4 tsp.	1 mL

Combine first 3 ingredients in small cup. Sprinkle over both sides of turkey.

Heat 1 tsp. (5 mL) of first amount of cooking oil in large frying pan on medium-high. Cook turkey, in 3 batches, for about 45 seconds per side, adding more oil if necessary, until no longer pink inside. Transfer to large plate. Cover to keep warm.

Heat second amount of cooking oil in same pan. Add remaining 10 ingredients. Cook for about 6 minutes, stirring often, until vegetables are tender-crisp. Transfer to serving dish. Arrange turkey over top. Serves 4.

1 serving: 249 Calories; 9.0 g Total Fat (4.2 g Mono, 2.3 g Poly, 0.6 g Sat); 45 mg Cholesterol; 15 g Carbohydrate; 5 g Fibre; 30 g Protein; 511 mg Sodium

fish in black bean sauce

This light Asian stir-fry is a perfect match for steamed rice.

Sesame (or cooking) oil	1 tsp.	5 mL
Firm white-fleshed fish (such as cod or halibut), cut into bite-sized pieces	1 lb.	454 g
Medium onion, slivered lengthwise	1	1
Minced ginger root	2 tsp.	10 mL
Garlic clove, minced	1	1
Large red pepper, cut into chunks	1	1
Large yellow pepper, cut into chunks	1	1
Sliced fresh white mushrooms	2 cups	500 mL
Snow peas, trimmed	2 cups	500 mL
Water	1/4 cup	60 mL
Black bean sauce (pourable)	1/4 cup	60 mL
Cold water	1 tbsp.	15 mL
Low-sodium soy sauce	1 tbsp.	15 mL
Granulated sugar	2 tsp.	10 mL
Cornstarch	2 tsp.	10 mL

Heat wok or large frying pan on medium-high until very hot. Add sesame oil. Add fish. Stir-fry for 2 minutes. Add next 3 ingredients. Stir-fry for 2 minutes. Transfer to plate.

Add next 5 ingredients to same wok. Stir-fry for 2 minutes.

Stir next 4 ingredients into cornstarch in small cup. Add to vegetables. Stir-fry for about 2 minutes until vegetables are tender-crisp and sauce is thickened. Add fish and onion. Stir gently. Makes about 6 cups (1.5 L).

1 cup (250 mL): 125 Calories; 2.0 g Total Fat (0 g Mono, 0.5 g Poly, 0 g Sat); 33 mg Cholesterol; 12 g Carbohydrate; 2 g Fibre; 16 g Protein; 231 mg Sodium

mexican basa-stuffed peppers

These deliciously different stuffed peppers are filled with a spicy blend of fish, rice and vegetables.

Chili powder	1 tbsp.	15 mL
Ground cumin	1 tbsp.	15 mL
Salt	1 tsp.	5 mL
Basa fillets, any small bones removed	1 lb.	454 g
Cooking oil	1 tbsp.	15 mL
Cooking oil	1 tsp.	5 mL
Finely chopped onion	1/2 cup	125 mL
Can of diced tomatoes, drained	14 oz.	398 mL
Cooked long-grain white rice (about 1/3 cup, 75 mL, uncooked)	1 cup	250 mL
Garlic cloves, minced (or 1/2 tsp., 2 mL, powder)	2	2
Finely chopped fresh jalapeño pepper (see Tip, page 64)	1 tsp.	5 mL
Large red peppers, halved lengthwise	2	2
Water	1/2 cup	125 mL

Combine first 3 ingredients in small bowl. Rub on both sides of fillets.

Heat first amount of cooking oil in large frying pan on medium. Add fillets. Cook for about 3 minutes per side until starting to brown. Transfer to cutting board. Cut into bite-sized pieces.

Heat second amount of cooking oil in same frying pan. Add onion. Cook for about 5 minutes, stirring often, until softened.

Add next 4 ingredients and fish. Stir. Remove from heat.

Arrange red pepper halves in ungreased 2 quart (2 L) casserole. Spoon fish mixture into peppers. Pour water into casserole. Bake, covered, in 350°F (175°C) oven for about 30 minutes until red peppers are tender-crisp. Transfer with slotted spoon to serving plates. Makes 4 stuffed peppers.

1 stuffed pepper: 252 Calories; 9.9 g Total Fat (2.7 g Mono, 1.5 g Poly, 2.1 g Sat); 51 mg Cholesterol; 22 g Carbohydrate; 3 g Fibre; 18 g Protein; 876 mg Sodium

make-ahead breakfast bake

One of those fantastic breakfast dishes that you chill overnight and bake in the morning—perfect for an early group of hungry guests!

Texas bread loaf, crusts removed and cut into 1 inch (2.5 cm) cubes	1/2	1/2
Small red peppers, chopped	2	2
Grated Cheddar cheese	1/2 cup	125 mL
Bacon slices, cooked crisp and crumbled	6	6
Green onions, chopped	4	4
Large eggs, fork-beaten	8	8
Milk	2 cups	500 mL
Chopped fresh basil	1/4 cup	60 mL
Mayonnaise	2 tbsp.	30 mL
Dry mustard	1 tsp.	5 mL
Salt, sprinkle		
Pepper, sprinkle		

Arrange bread cubes in bottom of greased deep 3 quart (3 L) baking dish. Sprinkle with next 4 ingredients.

Combine remaining 7 ingredients in medium bowl. Pour evenly over bread cubes. Chill, covered, for at least 8 hours or overnight. Bake, uncovered, in 350°F (175°C) oven for 50 to 60 minutes until set and golden. Serves 6.

1 serving: 312 Calories; 17.0 g Total Fat (6.0 g Mono, 4.0 g Poly, 6.0 g Sat); 206 mg Cholesterol; 22 g Carbohydrate; 2 g Fibre; 18 g Protein; 450 mg Sodium

pork and peppers

A satisfying stir-fry with tender pork and oodles of peppers.

Cooking oil	1 tbsp.	15 mL
Pork tenderloin, thinly sliced	1 1/2 lbs.	680 g
Chopped green pepper (about 2 medium)	1 1/2 cups	375 mL
Chopped red pepper (about 2 medium)	1 1/2 cups	375 mL
Chopped yellow pepper (about 2 medium)	1 1/2 cups	375 mL
Green onions, cut into 3 inch (7.5 cm) pieces	6	6
Sake (rice wine) or dry sherry	1/4 cup	60 mL
Soy sauce	1/4 cup	60 mL
Granulated sugar	2 tbsp.	30 mL
Cornstarch	1 tbsp.	15 mL

Heat wok or large frying pan on medium-high until very hot. Add cooking oil. Add pork. Stir-fry for about 2 minutes until browned.

Add next 4 ingredients. Stir-fry for about 6 minutes until peppers are tender-crisp.

Stir next 3 ingredients into cornstarch in small bowl until smooth. Add to pork mixture. Heat and stir until boiling and thickened. Serves 6.

1 serving: 249 Calories; 9.0 g Total Fat (4.0 g Mono, 1.5 g Poly, 2.5 g Sat); 75 mg Cholesterol; 14 g Carbohydrate; 2 g Fibre; 26 g Protein; 672 mg Sodium

sausage pepper skillet

Round out this hearty and colourful skillet with cheesy polenta or couscous.

Olive (or cooking) oil	2 tsp.	10 mL
Hot Italian sausage, cut into 1 inch (2.5 cm) pieces	1 lb.	454 g
Sliced green pepper	1 1/2 cups	375 mL
Sliced red pepper	1 1/2 cups	375 mL
Sliced yellow pepper	1 1/2 cups	375 mL
Sliced red onion	3/4 cup	175 mL
Prepared chicken broth	1/2 cup	125 mL
Balsamic vinegar	3 tbsp.	50 mL
Sun-dried tomatoes, softened in boiling water for 10 minutes before chopping	2 tbsp.	30 mL

Heat olive oil in large frying pan on medium. Add sausage. Cook for 6 to 8 minutes, stirring often, until browned. Transfer with slotted spoon to paper towels to drain. Drain and discard all but 2 tsp. (10 mL) drippings.

Heat drippings in same frying pan. Add next 4 ingredients. Stir. Cook, covered, for 5 to 10 minutes, stirring occasionally, until onion is softened and peppers are tender-crisp.

Add remaining 3 ingredients and sausage. Heat and stir for about 5 minutes, scraping any brown bits from bottom of pan, until heated through. Makes about 6 cups (1.5 L). Serves 4.

1 serving: 460 Calories; 32.7 g Total Fat (15.6 g Mono, 4.3 g Poly, 11.0 g Sat); 90 mg Cholesterol; 16 g Carbohydrate; 3 g Fibre; 26 g Protein; 1190 mg Sodium

couscous-stuffed peppers

A delicious main course, these peppers are stuffed with whole-wheat couscous, cranberries and mushrooms. To make it a vegetarian meal, use vegetable broth in place of chicken broth.

Large yellow peppers, halved lengthwise	2	2
Prepared chicken broth	1 cup	250 mL
Whole-wheat couscous	1/2 cup	125 mL
Dried cranberries	1/3 cup	75 mL
Curry powder	1/2 tsp	2 mL
Ground cumin	1/4 tsp.	1 mL
Cooking oil	1 tsp.	5 mL
Chopped onion	1/2 cup	125 mL
Sliced fresh white mushrooms	1/2 cup	125 mL
Garlic clove, minced (or 1/4 tsp., 1 mL, powder)	1	1
Canned chickpeas (garbanzo beans), rinsed and drained	1 cup	250 mL
Curry powder	1/2 tsp.	2 mL
Ground cumin	1/8 tsp.	0.5 mL
Salt	1/8 tsp.	0.5 mL
Pepper	1/8 tsp.	0.5 mL

Place yellow pepper halves, cut-side down, on greased baking sheet with sides. Bake in 450°F (230°C) oven for 12 to 15 minutes until tender-crisp.

Measure broth into medium saucepan. Bring to a boil. Add next 4 ingredients. Stir. Remove from heat. Let stand, covered, for about 5 minutes until liquid is absorbed. Fluff with fork. Cover to keep warm.

Heat cooking oil in medium frying pan on medium. Add next 3 ingredients. Cook for about 5 minutes, stirring often, until onion starts to soften.

Add remaining 5 ingredients. Stir. Cook, covered, for about 5 minutes until heated through. Add to couscous mixture. Stir well. Spoon into pepper halves. Serves 4.

1 serving: 324 Calories; 5.1 g Total Fat (1.5 g Mono, 1.8 g Poly, 0.5 g Sat); 0 mg Cholesterol; 60 g Carbohydrate; 9 g Fibre; 14 g Protein; 461 mg Sodium

pepper and kale linguine

Simple and elegant vegetarian pasta made with nutritious kale and whole-wheat linguine.

Water	12 cups	3 L
Salt	1 1/2 tsp.	7 mL
Whole-wheat linguine	10 oz.	285 g
Chopped kale leaves, lightly packed (see Tip, page 64)	6 cups	1.5 L
Olive (or cooking) oil	1 tsp.	5 mL
Thinly sliced onion	1 cup	250 mL
Garlic cloves, minced (or 1/2 tsp., 2 mL, powder)	2	2
Thinly sliced orange pepper	2 cups	500 mL
Thinly sliced yellow pepper	2 cups	500 mL
Orange juice	1/2 cup	125 mL
Rice vinegar	2 tbsp.	30 mL
Soy sauce	2 tbsp.	30 mL
Ground ginger	1 tsp.	5 mL
Pepper	1/4 tsp.	1 mL
Water	1 tbsp.	15 mL
Cornstarch	1 tbsp.	15 mL

Combine water and salt in Dutch oven. Bring to a boil. Add pasta. Boil, uncovered, for 7 minutes, stirring occasionally. Add kale. Stir. Cook, uncovered, for about 3 minutes until pasta is tender but firm and kale is tender. Drain, reserving 1/2 cup (125 mL) cooking water. Return pasta and kale to same pot. Cover to keep warm.

Heat olive oil in large frying pan on medium. Add onion and garlic. Cook for 5 to 10 minutes, stirring often, until onion is softened.

Add next 7 ingredients and reserved cooking water. Stir. Bring to a boil. Cook for about 3 minutes, stirring occasionally, until peppers are tender-crisp.

Stir water into cornstarch in small cup. Add to pepper mixture. Heat and stir for 1 to 2 minutes until boiling and slightly thickened. Add to pasta mixture. Toss. Makes about 8 cups (2 L).

1 cup (250 mL): 197 Calories; 1.8 g Total Fat (0.5 g Mono, 0.4 g Poly, 0.3 g Sat); 0 mg Cholesterol; 39 g Carbohydrate; 4 g Fibre; 8 g Protein; 353 mg Sodium

roasted red pepper pizza

Sometimes the best pizzas are those made with minimal toppings. This pizza is a simple combination of veggies, cheese and fresh basil.

Prebaked pizza crust (12 inch, 30 cm, diameter)	1	1
Pizza sauce	1/3 cup	75 mL
Chopped roasted red peppers	1 cup	250 mL
Fresh spinach leaves, lightly packed	1 cup	250 mL
Thinly sliced red onion	1 cup	250 mL
Chopped fresh basil (or 1 1/2 tsp., 7 mL, dried)	2 tbsp.	30 mL
Crumbled light feta cheese (about 2 oz., 57 g)	1/3 cup	75 mL
Grated Parmesan cheese	3 tbsp.	50 mL

Place pizza crust on ungreased 12 inch (30 cm) pizza pan or baking sheet. Spread pizza sauce evenly over crust.

Layer remaining 6 ingredients, in order given, over sauce. Bake on lowest rack in 475°F (240°C) oven for about 20 minutes until crust is browned. Cuts into 8 wedges.

1 wedge: 145 Calories; 3.9 g Total Fat (0.8 g Mono, 0.2 g Poly, 1.6 g Sat); 5 mg Cholesterol; 21 g Carbohydrate; 1 g Fibre; 6 g Protein; 304 mg Sodium

pepper stir-fry

For this stir-fry prepared on the grill, ensure that the handle of your pan is heatproof, or use a cast iron pan (and oven mitts!).

Cooking oil	2 tbsp.	30 mL
Small red onion, sliced	1	1
Sliced celery	1 cup	250 mL
Large green pepper, cut into strips	1	1
Large red pepper, diced	1	1
Large yellow pepper, cut into strips	1	1
Medium zucchini (with peel), cut into short fingers	1	1
Fresh bean sprouts	1/2 cup	125 mL
Salt, sprinkle		
Pepper, sprinkle		
Slivered almonds, toasted (see Tip, page 64), for garnish		

Preheat gas barbecue to medium-high. Heat cooking oil in wok or large frying pan on grill. Add onion and celery. Stir-fry for 5 minutes.

Add next 4 ingredients. Stir-fry for about 5 minutes until peppers are tender-crisp.

Add bean sprouts. Stir-fry until heated through. Sprinkle with salt and pepper.

Garnish with almonds. Serves 4.

1 serving: 110 Calories; 7.0 g Total Fat (4.0 g Mono, 2.0 g Poly, 0.5 g Sat); 0 mg Cholesterol; 12 g Carbohydrate; 3 g Fibre; 3 g Protein; 34 mg Sodium

sweet peppers and almonds

Crunchy nuts are perfectly paired with colourful peppers and caramelized onion in this tempting side dish.

Cooking oil	1 tbsp.	15 mL
Thinly sliced onion	1 1/2 cups	375 mL
Balsamic vinegar	2 tbsp.	30 mL
Brown sugar, packed	2 tbsp.	30 mL
Sliced green pepper	1 cup	250 mL
Sliced red pepper	1 cup	250 mL
Sliced yellow pepper	1 cup	250 mL
Sliced natural almonds, toasted (see Tip, page 64)	1/2 cup	125 mL

Heat cooking oil in large frying pan on medium. Add onion. Cook for about 10 minutes, stirring occasionally, until caramelized.

Add vinegar and brown sugar. Heat and stir for 1 to 2 minutes until sugar is dissolved.

Add next 3 ingredients. Cook for about 5 minutes, stirring occasionally, until peppers are tender-crisp.

Add almonds. Stir. Makes about 2 1/2 cups (625 mL).

1/2 cup (125 mL): 146 Calories; 7.8 g Total Fat (4.7 g Mono, 2.1 g Poly, 0.6 g Sat); 0 mg Cholesterol; 18 g Carbohydrate; 3 g Fibre; 3 g Protein; 8 mg Sodium

antipasto salad

This salad is chock full of healthy veggies and chickpeas—perfect for serving on the patio in the summertime! Switch up any of the vegetables in this versatile salad with thinly sliced zucchini, sliced fresh mushrooms, olives or tomatoes.

Can of condensed chicken broth	10 oz.	284 mL
White wine vinegar	3/4 cup	175 mL
Cornstarch	2 tsp.	10 mL
Dried basil	2 tsp.	10 mL
Dried oregano	2 tsp.	10 mL
Garlic cloves, crushed	2	2
Granulated sugar	1 tsp.	5 mL
Broccoli florets	2 cups	500 mL
Can of artichoke hearts, drained and quartered	14 oz.	398 mL
Can of chickpeas (garbanzo beans), rinsed and drained	19 oz.	540 mL
Can of solid white tuna in water, drained and flaked	6 oz.	170 g
Medium green pepper, cut into 1/4 inch (6 mm) slices	1	1
Medium red pepper, cut into 1/4 inch (6 mm) slices	1	1
Medium yellow pepper, cut into 1/4 inch (6 mm) slices	1	1
Small red onion, thinly sliced	1	1

Combine first 7 ingredients in medium saucepan. Heat and stir until boiling and slightly thickened.

Add broccoli. Stir. Remove from heat. Cool to room temperature.

Combine remaining 7 ingredients in large bowl. Add broccoli mixture. Toss well. Chill for at least 6 hours or overnight, stirring occasionally. Just before serving, stir salad and drain dressing. Makes about 10 cups (2.5 L).

1 cup (250 mL): 90 Calories; 1.5 g Total Fat (0 g Mono, 0 g Poly, 0 g Sat); 7 mg Cholesterol; 12 g Carbohydrate; 3 g Fibre; 8 g Protein; 414 mg Sodium

chipotle red pepper soup

Chipotle peppers add a special smoky heat to this smooth soup.

Olive (or cooking) oil	1 tsp.	5 mL
Chopped onion	1 cup	250 mL
Garlic cloves, minced (or 1/2 tsp., 2 mL, powder)	2	2
Chopped chipotle peppers in adobo sauce (see Tip, page 64)	1 tsp.	5 mL
Prepared vegetable broth	2 1/2 cups	625 mL
Jar of roasted red peppers (with liquid)	14 oz.	398 mL
Granulated sugar	2 tsp.	10 mL
Half-and-half cream	1/2 cup	125 mL
Grated orange zest	1 tsp.	5 mL
Salt	1/2 tsp.	2 mL
Pepper	1/4 tsp.	1 mL

Heat olive oil in large saucepan on medium. Add next 3 ingredients. Cook, uncovered, for 5 to 10 minutes, stirring occasionally, until onion is softened.

Add next 3 ingredients. Stir. Bring to a boil. Reduce heat to medium-low. Simmer, uncovered, for 5 minutes to blend flavours. Carefully process with hand blender or in blender until smooth (see Safety Tip).

Add remaining 4 ingredients. Stir. Makes about 4 3/4 cups (1.2 L). Serves 6.

1 serving: 148 Calories; 3.4 g Total Fat (1.3 g Mono, 0.2 g Poly, 1.6 g Sat); 8 mg Cholesterol; 19 g Carbohydrate; 1 g Fibre; 4 g Protein; 1061 mg Sodium

Safety Tip: Follow manufacturer's instructions for processing hot liquids.

sweet pepper soup

When red peppers are plentiful, make this deliciously vibrant soup.

Chopped red pepper (about 10 medium)	7 cups	1.75 L
Chopped onion	2 cups	500 mL
Water	2 cups	500 mL
Chicken bouillon powder	1/4 cup	60 mL
Milk	3 1/2 cups	875 mL
Salt	1 tsp.	5 mL
Pepper	1/4 tsp.	1 mL
Dried thyme	1/4 tsp.	1 mL
Water	3 tbsp.	50 mL
Cornstarch	2 tbsp.	30 mL

Combine first 4 ingredients in large saucepan. Bring to a boil. Reduce heat to medium-low. Simmer, covered, for about 20 minutes until peppers and onion are tender. Cool slightly. Carefully process with hand blender, or in blender in batches, until smooth (see Safety Tip). Transfer to large bowl. Cover to keep warm.

Combine next 4 ingredients in same large saucepan. Bring to a boil. Add red pepper mixture. Return to a boil.

Stir water into cornstarch in small cup. Add to red pepper mixture. Heat and stir until boiling and thickened. Makes about 8 cups (2 L).

1 cup (250 mL): 120 Calories; 2.0 g Total Fat (0 g Mono, 0 g Poly, 1.0 g Sat); 5 mg Cholesterol; 20 g Carbohydrate; 3 g Fibre; 7 g Protein; 924 mg Sodium

Safety Tip: Follow manufacturer's instructions for processing hot liquids.

recipe index

topical tips

Chopping hot peppers: Hot peppers contain capsaicin in the seeds and ribs. Remove the seeds and ribs to reduce the heat. Wear gloves when handling hot peppers. Do not touch your face near eyes.

Cutting and storing kale: To remove the centre rib from kale, fold the leaf in half along the rib and then cut along the length of the rib. To store, place leaves in large freezer bag. Once frozen, crumble in bag.

Handling chipotle peppers: Chipotle chili peppers are smoked jalapeño peppers. Wash your hands after handling. To store any leftover chipotle peppers, divide into recipe-friendly portions and freeze, with sauce, in airtight containers for up to 1 year.

Making soured milk: If a recipe calls for soured milk, measure 1 tbsp. (15 mL) white vinegar or lemon juice into a 1 cup (250 mL) liquid measure. Add enough milk to make 1 cup (250 mL). Stir. Let stand for 1 minute.

Toasting nuts, seeds or coconut: Cooking times will vary for each ingredient, so never toast them together. For small amounts, place ingredient in an ungreased frying pan. Heat on medium for 3 to 5 minutes, stirring often, until golden. For larger amounts, spread ingredient evenly in an ungreased shallow pan. Bake in a 350°F (175°C) oven for 5 to 10 minutes, stirring or shaking often, until golden.

Tomato paste leftovers: If a recipe calls for less than an entire can of tomato paste, freeze the unopened can for 30 minutes. Open both ends and push the contents through one end. Slice off only what you need. Freeze the remaining paste in a resealable freezer bag or plastic wrap for future use.

Nutrition Information Guidelines

Each recipe is analyzed using the Canadian Nutrient File from Health Canada, which is based on the United States Department of Agriculture (USDA) Nutrient Database.

- If more than one ingredient is listed (such as "butter or hard margarine"), or if a range is given (1 – 2 tsp., 5 – 10 mL), only the first ingredient or first amount is analyzed.

- Ingredients indicating "sprinkle," "optional" or "for garnish" are not included in the nutrition information.

- Milk used is 1% M.F. (milk fat),unless otherwise stated.

- Cooking oil used is canola oil, unless otherwise stated.

- For meat, poultry and fish, the serving size per person is based on the recommended 4 oz. (113 g) uncooked weight (without bone), which is 2 – 3 oz. (57 – 85 g) cooked weight (without bone)— approximately the size of a deck of playing cards.

- The fat in recipes and combination foods can vary greatly depending on the sources and types of fats used in each specific ingredient. For these reasons, the count of saturated, monounsaturated and polyunsaturated fats may not add up to the total fat content.